CREATE with
DUCT
TAPE

DUCT TAPE
Animals

by Carolyn Bernhardt

Lerner Publications ◆ Minneapolis

Lerner Publications Company
A division of Lerner Publishing Group, Inc.
241 First Avenue North
Minneapolis, MN 55401 USA

For reading levels and more information, look up this title at www.lernerbooks.com.

Main body text set in Bembo. Typeface provided by Monotype.

Library of Congress Cataloging-in-Publication Data

Names: Bernhardt, Carolyn, author.
Title: Duct tape animals / by Carolyn Bernhardt.
Description: Minneapolis, MN : Lerner Publications, [2016] | Series: Create with duct tape | Audience: Ages 7-11. | Audience: Grades 4 to 6. | Includes bibliographical references and index.
Identifiers: LCCN 2016018667 (print) | LCCN 2016020250 (ebook) | ISBN 9781512426687 (lb : alk. paper) | ISBN 9781512427653 (eb pdf)
Subjects: LCSH: Tape craft--Juvenile literature. | Duct tape--Juvenile literature. | Handicraft--Juvenile literature.
Classification: LCC TT869.7 .B46922 2016 (print) | LCC TT869.7 (ebook) | DDC 745.59--dc23

LC record available at https://lccn.loc.gov/2016018667

Manufactured in the United States of America
1-41434-23339-8/16/2016

Contents

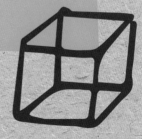

Beastly Strong Tape

What has the strength to repair cars but can be ripped with bare hands? It's sticky and often silvery. It's duct tape!

This supertough tape was first known as duck tape. During World War II (1939–1945), soldiers used the tape to protect their weapons. It was **waterproof**, just like a duck's feathers. It could also repair military vehicles. News of this tough tape spread. People began using it in everyday life. It was very good for connecting **air ducts**. Soon, people started calling it duct tape.

Today, people patch, bind, and repair many things with duct tape. They also create tools, toys, clothing, and **accessories**. Some people even use it to create art! Imagine awesome animal art made entirely from tape. Dream up a rainbow of colorful wings, stuffed statues tough enough to play with, and roaring beasts with pointy tape teeth. Gather duct tape rolls with wild prints and get ready to create some duct tape animals!

Before You Get Started

Sticky Supply

Crafting with duct tape is fun and simple. Many crafts can be made with only one roll! Because duct tape is so sticky, no buttons or pins are needed. You can simply stick ears, eyes, limbs, and more right onto your animals. However, duct tape's stickiness can make it challenging to work with too. This tape can easily flop and twist, sticking to itself or to other objects. The key to using duct tape is to take your time! Working slowly and carefully will help your projects turn out the best they can be.

Setting Up a Workspace

Duct tape crafts may not require many tools or extra supplies. But creating a clean workspace is still important. Clear your space of any garbage. Make sure tools and small supplies are neatly stored away from surfaces where you will be handling tape. This will prevent them from getting stuck on the tape. Duct tape can be hard to remove from certain surfaces. It may also leave a sticky **residue** behind. So check with an adult first to make sure you have permission to stick tape to the table's surface.

Fierce Fibers

Duct tape is super strong. This strength comes from the tape's special fibers. These fibers are woven into the tape in a crisscross pattern. The fibers placed in this pattern keep the duct tape secure even under pressure.

Wild Tape Things

Animal art is all about being creative! The creatures you craft don't need to look realistic. They can have wild colors, crazy patterns, or superhuge features. Duct tape makes it easy to build and add extra features. So as you create these critters, use your imagination. What would those wings look like if you made them supersized? Could you turn a cute duct tape rabbit into a fearsome beast with pointy teeth? Try it out! Have fun and make each wild tape thing in your own style!

Stay Safe

Any time you use duct tape, safety is most important. Never stick duct tape's sticky side directly to skin. Do not place duct tape on your or someone else's face. Never place it over eyes, ears, or mouths. And never bind any body part with duct tape. Finally, be careful when using sharp objects, such as scissors. Always check in with an adult before working on the crafts in this book.

Striped
Tape Snake

String together a
slithering striped snake!

Materials

- scissors
- yarn
- measuring tape
- duct tape
- optional: hot glue and
  hot glue gun, googly
  eyes, permanent
  markers

Sticky Tip

To make a braid, divide the
yarn into three groups. Cross the
right group over the middle group.
Cross the left group over the
middle group. Repeat! Secure the
end with more yarn.

1 Cut thirty strands of yarn as long as your **arm span**. Gather the strands together. Tie a short piece of yarn around one end. Separate three groups of ten yarn strands. Braid the yarn. Tie a short piece of yarn around the end.

2

2 Fold one end of the braid down about 4 inches (10 centimeters). Tie this end to the rest of the braid with a short piece of yarn. This will be the head.

3

3 Wrap the snake in duct tape. Wrap the end extra tight to make a narrow tail.

4 Design the snake's face however you want! With adult help, hot glue on googly eyes. Or, draw its face with permanent markers. Then attach a tape tongue to its mouth.

5 Decorate the snake's body with different colors of tape. Place your sticky snake creation in sneaky spots to give friends or family quite a surprise!

5

Tube Tape Pet

Transform toilet paper tubes into tiny pets with some duct tape magic!

Materials

- toilet paper tube
- duct tape
- scissors
- measuring tape
- permanent marker
- optional: googly eyes, hot glue and hot glue gun

Sticky Tip

Does your animal need some wild, rolling eyes? With adult help, hot glue googly eyes onto the animal's face. It will bring your tube pet to life!

1

1. Select an animal to make. It could be anything from an owl to an elephant! Hold the tube vertically in your hands. Fold the top edges of the tube in toward the center. This will form two points on either side.

2. Cover the tube in duct tape.

3. Cut six strips of duct tape 10 inches (25.4 cm) long. Overlap the long edge of one strip slightly with the long edge of another strip. Keep them sticky-side up. Repeat with the remaining strips until you've formed a rectangular tape sheet.

3

4. Cover the rectangle with more duct tape strips, pressing the sticky sides together. Then draw the animal's body parts on the duct tape sheet. Cut them out.

5. Secure the animal's body parts onto the tube with more tape.

6. Draw the finishing touches on the animal. You can add spots or stripes. Or, tape on a pointy pair of horns. Take care of your tube creatures just as you would a favorite pet!

4

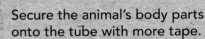

Sticky-Legged Spider

Create a creepy-crawly companion by latching long legs to a round ball body!

Materials

- bendy straws
- measuring tape
- scissors
- foam ball
- duct tape
- hot glue and hot glue gun
- googly eyes

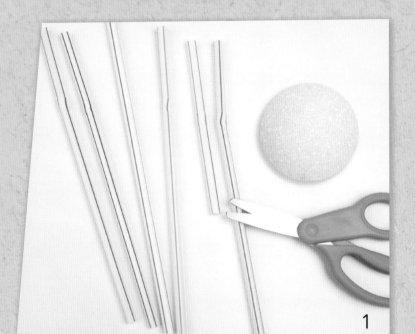

1

 1 Trim eight bendy straws 5 inches (12.7 cm) long. Do not cut the bends off. Insert the straws into the foam ball. These will be the spider's legs.

 2 Cover the ball with duct tape. This will be the spider's body.

 3 Cover the straws with duct tape.

 4 With an adult's help, hot glue googly eyes onto the spider's face. This scurrying spider will keep its creepy eyes on you at all times!

2

Did You Know?

When doubled over itself, a single strip of duct tape can pull more than 1 ton (907.2 kilograms).

3

Sculpted
Scrap
Rabbit

Sculpt spare strips into a
fun patchwork bunny!

Materials

- leftover duct tape
- pen
- cardboard
- scissors
- pom-pom
- googly eyes
- double-stick tape

1 **Crumple** up some of your leftover tape into a ball for the head. Make a larger ball for the body.

1

2 Attach the head to the body with duct tape. Cover the whole body with duct tape.

2

3 Draw the rabbit's back leg and foot on the cardboard. Cut it out. Trace the shape on cardboard and cut it out. Cover both legs with scrap strips. Attach them to the body.

4 Cut two strips of duct tape. Lay one on top of the other, pressing the sticky sides together. Draw two ears on the strip. Cut them out. Draw two inner ear shapes on a new strip of tape. Cut them out and stick them in the center of each ear. Pinch the bottoms of the ears and attach them to the sides of the head.

5 Make two small front paws and attach with duct tape.

6 Use double-stick tape to attach the pom-pom tail and the googly eyes.

3

Tape Tortoise

Use bits of bright tape to build a supercool shell!

Materials

- small paper plate
- scissors
- duct tape
- measuring tape
- optional: hot glue and hot glue gun, googly eyes, permanent marker

1 Turn the plate upside down. Trim the upturned edge off of the plate.

2 Cover the plate with duct tape.

3 Cut two strips of tape 4 inches (10 cm) long. Fold the ends of the strips halfway, leaving a sticky portion on each strip. Then cut them in half the long way to make four thin strips. These are the tortoise's legs. Create one more strip for the tail.

4 Trim the corners off the legs, giving them a rounded shape. Trim the tail into a point. Attach the legs and tail to the underside of the tortoise.

5 Cut a 3-inch (7.6 cm) strip of duct tape. Fold one end halfway up. Keep the sticky sides touching. This is the tortoise's head. Attach it to the body. Trim it to be rounded like a real-life tortoise's head.

6 Attach googly eyes or draw a face to bring this tape tortoise to life!

Roaring Tape Ring

Bring a duct tape ring roaring to life with enormous eyes and fierce fangs!

Materials

- marker
- cardboard
- scissors
- duct tape
- Optional: hot glue and hot glue gun, googly eyes, cardboard tube

1

 1 Draw a large circle on the cardboard and cut it out. Cut a smaller circle inside the big circle to form a large ring. Cover the ring in duct tape.

2 Cut ten strips of duct tape. Fold the ends of the strips the short way, leaving a sticky portion on each strip. These are the animal's teeth. Round off their edges or trim them into points.

 3 Attach the teeth to the animal's mouth.

 4 Decorate your roaring beast! Attach wild googly eyes, a cardboard-tube horn, or a flowing duct tape mane. Then hang the animal on the door to your room. Welcome visitors with a fearsome roar!

2

3

Did You Know?

In 2014, the company 3M made special animal-print duct tape. The prints were based on animals from the Wildcat Sanctuary of Minnesota.

Floating
Shark Fin

Tape together a freaky fin that lives in tubs and terrifies bathers!

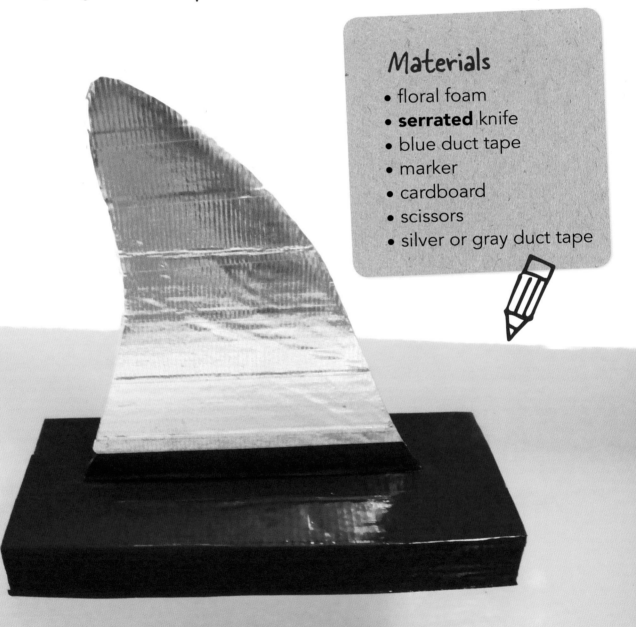

Materials
- floral foam
- **serrated** knife
- blue duct tape
- marker
- cardboard
- scissors
- silver or gray duct tape

1

2

3

With adult help, cut a rectangle out of the foam using a serrated knife. This is the fin's base. Cover it in blue duct tape.

2 Draw a fin shape on the cardboard. The bottom of the fin should be no wider than the base is long. Cut out the fin.

3 Cover the fin in silver or gray duct tape.

4 Tape the fin to its base with blue duct tape.

5 Float your fin in a tub or pool and watch people squirm at the shark sighting!

Duct Tape
Dragonfly

Design a duct tape dragonfly with wings as stunning as they are sturdy!

Materials

- scissors
- measuring tape
- duct tape
- permanent marker
- toilet paper tube
- (optional: hot glue and hot glue gun, googly eyes)

1. Cut sixteen strips of duct tape 12 inches (30.5 cm) long. Overlap the long edge of one strip slightly with the long edge of another strip. Keep them sticky-side up. Repeat with the remaining strips until you've formed a sheet. Fold the duct tape sheet in half the long way, pressing the sticky sides together.

2. Draw dragonfly wings on the duct tape sheet. Cut them out. Decorate both sides of the wings with bright strips of tape.

3. Tape the wings together by attaching a strip of duct tape to the ends of the wings. Leave some space between them for the sticky side to show through.

4. Cut a slit along the side of the cardboard tube. Then roll it tightly. While keeping it rolled thin, cover it in duct tape. This is the dragonfly's body.

5. Press the body to the strip of tape that connects the wings.

6. Roll two tiny strips of duct tape into small tubes. Tape them to the dragonfly's head. These are its antennae. Attach googly eyes if you'd like. Your dragonfly friend is now ready to take flight. Flap and flutter its wings around the house for some fun!

Animal Head

This monstrous horned beast will bellow at guests from your wall!

Materials

- paper
- pencil
- scissors
- marker
- cardboard
- duct tape
- newspaper
- large paper clip

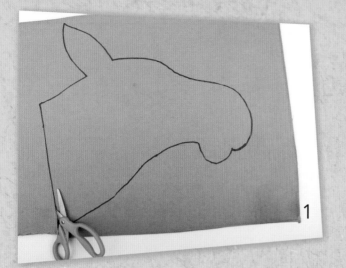

1

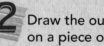

1 Think of an animal with horns. This could be a moose, deer, or a made-up monster! Draw the side view of the animal's face on paper. Tape two pieces of paper together if you need more space. Cut it out and trace it twice on cardboard. Cut out both cardboard shapes.

3

2 Draw the outline of one horn on a piece of paper. Cut it out.

3 Trace the horn on cardboard. Flip the paper horn horizontally. Trace the horn again. Make sure there is at least 3 inches (7.6 cm) in the center. Cut the horns out in one piece. Cover the horns in duct tape.

4 Cover the opposite sides of both face cutouts in duct tape. Cut a slot in the same location on each side of the face where the horns will go.

Animal Head continued next page

4

Animal Head, continued

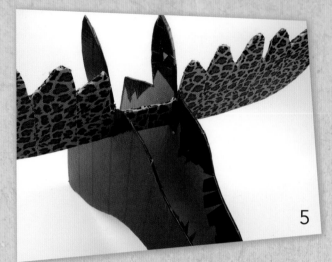

5

Insert the horns into the slots to connect the face cutouts. The faces should be 3 inches (7.6 cm) apart.

Begin wrapping duct tape across the space between the faces. When you are partway through, crumple some newspaper. Stuff the newspaper inside the head to keep the sides separated. Cover the remaining space with duct tape.

6

Draw a base for the head on cardboard. Cut it out. Tape the head to the base. Cover the base with duct tape.

7

Make a hanger by unfolding the halves of a large paper clip. Tape one half to the back of the base near the top. Use the other half to hang your horned head for all to admire!

Build Your Own
Duct
Tape Zoo

Each of your duct tape animals is unique! Put them on display in your own zoo or museum. Set up your room or backyard to show off the pets of your dreams. Which one is everyone's favorite? Which one is the creepiest? Head back to the duct tape drawing board and make as many more animals as you like until your zoo is packed with critters!

Cleanup and Safekeeping

Now that you've made these animals, it's time to clean up. Pick up all strips and put away your tools and supplies. Store duct tape rolls out of the sun. Throw away any ruined strips, or save them to create more crafts, such as the Sculpted Scrap Rabbit! To take care of your duct tape animals, store them away from direct heat or sunlight. Duct tape glue can become gummy if the tape gets too hot. If any of your animals become broken from wear, patch and repair them with more tape.

Keep Creating!

Duct tape can make some awesome animals. But these projects are just the beginning. What other creatures could you craft from this amazing tape? Imagine your own animal creations. Then tear, stick, and connect to bring them to life!

Glossary

accessories: small items that you wear with your clothes

air ducts: pipes that move air around buildings

arm span: the distance between the fingertips of one hand and the other when the arms are raised horizontally to the ground

crumple: to crush something into wrinkles and folds

residue: what remains after something else is removed or completed

serrated: having a blade like that of a saw

waterproof: designed to prevent water from entering

Further Information

Giggenbach, Ellen. *Papercraft Animals: 20 Creative & Colorful Model Projects to Fold and Display.*
Lake Forest, CA: Walter Foster Publishing, 2015.
From duct tape to paper: explore fun new animal crafts using another simple tool.

How Duck Tape® Was Named
http://duckbrand.com/about
Learn the history behind one of the most famous duct tape brands.

San Diego Zoo: Kids
http://kids.sandiegozoo.org
Play games, make fun crafts, and meet the many animals living at the San Diego Zoo!

Spelman, Lucy. *Animal Encyclopedia: 2,500 Animals with Photos, Maps, and More!*
Washington, DC: National Geographic, 2012.
This book brings you face-to-face with thousands of animals from around the world!

Index

Photo Acknowledgments

The images in this book are used with the permission of: © Feng Yu/Shutterstock Images, pp. 1 (top right), 4 (bottom), 7 (bottom), 8 (gray tape roll), 10 (bottom), 12 (bottom right), 29 (top right); © mama_mia/Shutterstock Images, pp. 3, 10, 12, 13, 14, 16, 18, 19, 20, 22, 24, 25, 26, 29, 30; © Mighty Media, Inc., pp. 1 (top), 1 (yellow tape), 2 (dark blue tape), 4 (leopard tape), 5 (yellow tape), 5 (lion craft), 5 (dark blue tape), 6 (orange tape), 7 (dark blue tape), 7 (leopard tape), 8 (dark blue tape), 8 (rabbit craft), 8 (yellow tape), 8 (orange tape), 9 (yellow tape), 10 (yellow tape), 10 (snake craft), 11 (yellow tape), 11 (top), 11 (middle), 11 (bottom), 12 (orange tape), 12 (tube pet crafts), 13 (orange tape), 13 (top), 13 (middle), 13 (bottom), 14 (light blue tape), 14 (spider craft), 15 (light blue tape), 15 (orange tape), 15 (top), 15 (middle), 15 (bottom), 16 (yellow tape), 16 (rabbit craft), 17 (yellow tape), 17 (orange tape), 17 (top), 17 (middle), 17 (bottom), 18 (orange tape), 18 (tortoise craft), 18 (pink tape), 19 (orange tape), 19 (top), 19 (middle), 19 (bottom), 20, 20 (lion craft), 20 (light blue tape), 21 (orange tape), 21 (top), 21 (light blue tape), 21 (middle), 21 (bottom), 22 (yellow tape), 22 (shark craft), 23 (yellow tape), 23 (top), 23 (middle), 23 (bottom), 24 (orange tape), 24 (tie-dye tape), 24 (dragonfly craft), 25 (orange tape), 25 (top), 25 (middle), 25 (bottom), 26 (light blue tape), 26 (animal head craft), 27 (light blue tape), 27 (top), 27 (middle), 27 (bottom), 28 (light blue tape), 28 (top), 28 (middle), 28 (bottom), 29 (yellow tape), 29 (orange tape), 29 (dark blue tape), 29 (leopard tape), 30 (leopard tape), 31 (yellow tape), 32 (yellow tape), 32 (dark blue tape); © Miodrag Gajic/iStockphoto, p. 9; © JoKMedia/iStockphoto, p. 6; © Tom Wang/Shutterstock Images, p. 29; © wongwean/Shutterstock Images, pp. 4 (blue paper), 6 (yellow paper), 11 (blue paper), 15 (yellow paper), 17 (blue paper), 21 (yellow paper), 23 (blue paper), 27 (yellow paper), 28 (yellow paper), 30 (blue paper).

Cover: © Feng Yu/Shutterstock Images (gray tape roll); © Mighty Media, Inc.; © wongwean/Shutterstock Images (yellow background).

Back Cover: © Feng Yu/Shutterstock Images (gray tape roll); © wongwean/Shutterstock Images (yellow background).